All You Know

By
Joyce A. Barnes

Illustrated by
Denny Bond

CELEBRATION PRESS
Pearson Learning Group

Contents

Cast of Characters 3

Scene 1:
The New Boy Routine 4

Scene 2:
¡Bienvenidos, Carlos! 8

Scene 3:
The Principal's Office 16

Scene 4:
Carlos the Goalie? 21

Scene 5:
Misconceptions 29

Scene 6:
We're a Team, Right? 36

Scene 7:
Carlos Tells the Truth 44

Scene 8:
Play the Game You Know 50

Glossary of Spanish Phrases . . . 56

Cast of Characters

Carlos Martinez

Roberto Martinez
Carlos's father

Dr. Isabel Martinez
Carlos's mother

Malcolm

Paul

Valerie

Cleo

Tasha

With

Mrs. Cabrero
teacher

Coach Jones
soccer coach

Mr. Boswell
school principal

Other Students

Scene 1
The New Boy Routine

(A family dining room. Carlos Martinez and his parents, Dr. Isabel Martinez and Roberto Martinez, sit around a table set for dinner. They pantomime eating during the scene.)

DR. MARTINEZ: Just think—this is our first meal in our new house.

MR. MARTINEZ: Yes, and the plates arrived just in time. I hope the rest of our belongings from Mexico will be here soon!

CARLOS: This chicken sure tastes good. I'm hungry from all that unpacking.

DR. MARTINEZ: It's hard to believe that you'll start

school on Monday, Carlos. We've barely settled in here.

CARLOS: I can wait to start school if you want.

DR. MARTINEZ: Oh, no, that's not what I meant! *(She looks at Carlos.)* You're not nervous about starting school, are you, *hijo*?

CARLOS: I wouldn't exactly say that I'm nervous. I'm definitely resigned, though. You know, this "new boy at school" routine is getting old.

MR. MARTINEZ: What do you mean, Carlos?

CARLOS: In the last three years, I've been the new boy at three different schools.

MR. MARTINEZ: *(thinks a moment)* Let's see: three years ago, before we moved to Mexico, you were in the third grade at Madison Elementary—just in the next town.

CARLOS: Those were the days. Playing baseball, going to Cub Scout meetings . . . I didn't have a care in the world.

MR. MARTINEZ: Then, right before your ninth birthday, I was transferred to Mexico City.

CARLOS: *(good-humoredly)* You mean *we* were transferred, Dad.

MR. MARTINEZ: That was definitely a family project. You both were real troupers, packing up and moving to a different country. It was easier for me— I was returning to my hometown.

CARLOS: That's when my misery as a new boy began.

DR. MARTINEZ: It wasn't that bad, was it, Carlos? At least you spoke a little Spanish.

CARLOS: Speaking it is one thing, and understanding it is something else. Suddenly everyone was speaking Spanish at top speed! I was lost for three months. All the television shows were in Spanish, all of the music. Teachers would say things to me in school, and I would just catch a few words.

MR. MARTINEZ: Okay, that was your first school in Mexico City. Then we bought our new house, and you transferred to Diego Rivera Grammar School.

CARLOS: That was new school number two. By then, I understood what people were saying, and I didn't always like it. *(mimicking a teasing manner)* "Hey, new kid! Where's your baseball hat?"

DR. MARTINEZ: Now, Carlos, I know you made some good friends at that school.

CARLOS: Oh, sure, Mom. I'm sure I'll make friends at Thomas Dewey Middle School, too. I'm also sure that I'll be in for more of the new boy routine. *(He pauses, trying to find the words that will make his parents understand.)* Let me explain the routine to you. First, everyone takes a good long look at you, without saying a word. This is just to figure out what's different about you so they can discuss it endlessly with their friends. There is *always* something different about you. It could be the way you talk or the way you wear your hair. In my case, it could be the fact that I come from somewhere else. Next, you have to work your way into their clubs and teams, all the things you took for granted at your old school. They don't accept you automatically. You have to prove yourself first, because you're new.

MR. MARTINEZ: Carlos, I know you'll adjust just as well here as you did in Mexico. You had a rough patch for a while there, not speaking the language well. That isn't going to be a problem here in the United States, though. Besides—here, you can play baseball again. It'll be easy for you.

CARLOS: I adjusted too well. Now I'm homesick for Mexico! I have friends there that I may never see again. I can't go to the *Museo Nacional de Antropología* and spend hours walking through the Aztec exhibits. You know how much I loved doing that, Dad. After three years in Mexico, I was beginning to feel as if it was home. Now, I'll have to learn how to be an American all over again.

DR. MARTINEZ: Okay, maybe it won't be so easy, Carlos. We know you're very adaptable, though. We're sure you can learn how to fit in here.

CARLOS: Sure, I can learn how to fit in. But what if it takes me three more years?

Scene 2

¡Bienvenidos, Carlos!

(A sixth-grade classroom, the following morning. Props can include a teacher's desk and chair, students' desks, a bookcase, a globe, and so on. The teacher's desk faces the audience, while the students' desks face each other on either side of the stage. In the front row, Valerie and Paul have moved over so that they are sitting on either side of Malcolm's desk. A book is open on the desk.)

MALCOLM: The way I see it, this was meant to happen. Our soccer goalkeeper moves away. Then, a month later, we get a new boy in school who comes from Mexico, where soccer is the national sport. It's serendipitous.

PAUL: Serendip—what?

MALCOLM: *(pronoucing it slowly)* Ser-en-dip-i-tous. It means something happened that we didn't expect, but it was just what we needed. It comes from the word *serendipity*.

PAUL: Oh. It sounds like something you eat.

VALERIE: Malcolm, just because Carlos is from Mexico City doesn't mean he plays soccer. Maybe he plays something else, like chess.

MALCOLM: Chess? Where'd you get that idea, Val?

VALERIE: I'm just saying that you shouldn't assume things about a person you've never met.

MALCOLM: I'm not assuming anything. I'm going to come right out and ask him when he gets to our class on Monday. So, come on, how do you say "Do you want to play on our soccer team?" in Spanish?

(In one corner, Tasha and Cleo are putting the finishing touches on a large, elaborate banner. Along with the words "¡Bienvenidos, Carlos!" written in large, colorful letters, the banner is decorated with photographs of Mexico City sites cut from magazines.)

TASHA: *(smoothing a picture in place on the banner and then standing back with Cleo to admire their work)* Does it need one more picture? Maybe another photograph of the National Palace?

CLEO: No, it's fine. But maybe I should shade a

little more yellow into the letters. What do you think, Tasha?

TASHA: I think the letters are beautiful just the way they are. It could use one more picture, though.

CLEO: No, the pictures are perfect. You don't need to add or change a thing. Which do you think Carlos will notice first, the words or the pictures?

TASHA: *(with false modesty)* Well, you know what they say: "A picture is worth a thousand words."

CLEO: *(getting a little upset)* Wait a minute! The words are in Spanish, Carlos's native language. He's sure to appreciate the fact that we're trying extra hard to make him feel welcome.

TASHA: Everyone expects to find words on a banner, Cleo!

MRS. CABRERO: *(standing and looking at her watch)* All right, class, we have about twenty minutes until the bell rings. Let's see how your preparations are coming along. Tasha, Cleo?

(The two girls hold up their elaborate banner.)

OTHER STUDENTS: *(applauding and calling out appreciative comments)* Way to go! Nice job!

CLEO: *(proudly)* The words ¡Bienvenidos, Carlos! say welcome to your new country, the United States of America.

TASHA: They also say how glad we are that you'll be in Mrs. Cabrero's homeroom and her Spanish

class with us here at Thomas Dewey Middle School.

PAUL: *(aside to Malcolm and Valerie)* Where does it say all of that?

TASHA: *(equally proud)* The pictures are to remind Carlos of his hometown, Mexico City.

MRS. CABRERO: Please tell us what the pictures show, Tasha.

TASHA: *(pointing to one of the images)* This is a monument in Chapultepec Park. The park is so big, it has forests and lakes, museums, and even a castle. Over here is the National Palace. Isn't it beautiful? Carlos is so lucky to have lived in Mexico City! It's filled with statues and artwork, and it has some of

11

the best museums in the entire world.

MRS. CABRERO: You've both done a terrific job. Can you find a place to hang the banner?

TASHA: Sure, Mrs. Cabrero. *(She and Cleo walk toward the front of the stage and tape the banner to the wall.)* Where do you think Carlos will sit, Cleo? I was hoping he'd sit next to me, near the window.

CLEO: Oh! I was hoping he'd sit next to me. Let's ask. *(She raises her hand.)*

MRS. CABRERO: Yes, Cleo?

CLEO: Where will Carlos sit, Mrs. Cabrero? There's an empty desk next to mine. I could interpret for him if you're speaking English and he doesn't understand!

MALCOLM: *(raising his hand and speaking at the same time)* Mrs. Cabrero, don't you think Carlos should sit with a member of the soccer team? I bet Carlos loves the game just as much as I do. You know, Mexico's professional league is one of the best. They've played in a dozen World Cup tournaments.

VALERIE: *(mutters)* Oh, brother. *(She raises her hand.)*

MRS. CABRERO: What do you think, Val?

VALERIE: I think we should let Carlos decide where he wants to sit.

MRS. CABRERO: I think that *is* the best solution. We'll ask Carlos where he'd like to sit. Now, let's practice the Spanish conversations we've been working on. Valerie, could you go first?

VALERIE: *Buenos días, Carlos. Me llamo Valerie. ¿Cómo estás?*

MRS. CABRERO: *Muy bien, gracias.* That was excellent, Val. Malcolm, could you say your conversational lines for the class?

MALCOLM: *(speaking rapidly) Hola, Carlos. Mi nombre es Malcolm. ¿Qué pasa, amigo? Muchas gusto.*

PAUL: It's *mucho*, not *muchas*.

MALCOLM: Right, *mucho gusto.* Nice to meet you. *(He sighs.)* All I really want to say is, "Will you play on our soccer team?" Mrs. Cabrero, help me translate: "Carlos, we have a chance to go to the regional tournament. We need a player like you on our team."

VALERIE: Don't you think that's making a big leap, Malcolm?

MALCOLM: What do you mean?

VALERIE: I want our team to go to the regionals, too, but we shouldn't go around making generalizations about other people because of where they live. That's like saying everyone from Alaska must be a good ice skater because there's a lot of ice there. Just because Carlos is from Mexico, you think he's such a great soccer player that he can save the

whole season for our school!

TASHA: Carlos will probably jump at the chance to join the soccer team.

OTHER STUDENTS: Yeah! He'll be great. Wow, I can't wait to see him play.

(Malcolm looks at the other students, nodding with a satisfied grin. Valerie just shakes her head. Paul raises his hand.)

MRS. CABRERO: Yes, Paul?

PAUL: I have an idea. Let's bring some Mexican food to homeroom for Carlos's first day. I know how to make guacamole!

(Some students like this idea; others don't. Val continues to shake her head.)

MRS. CABRERO: That's a generous thought, Paul, but let's not overwhelm Carlos on his first day with us. When he's been here a little longer, we can plan some activities that will help us all learn more about Mexico.

(The bell rings. Students pantomime packing up their backpacks. Some pretend to grab papers or books from their desks.)

MRS. CABRERO: That's all the time we have today. Don't forget to study for your vocabulary quiz next week!

MALCOLM: I still want to know how to say *soccer* in Spanish.

MRS. CABRERO: They call it *fútbol*.

OTHER STUDENTS: *¡Adiós, Señora Cabrero!*

MRS. CABRERO: *¡Adiós!*

MALCOLM: Really? Then what do they call football?

MRS. CABRERO: The American game of football is simply called football.

MALCOLM: *Gracias, Señora Cabrero.* Have a great day!

Scene 3
The Principal's Office

(The principal's office, Monday morning. The teacher's desk from Scene 2 is now the principal's desk. Two chairs are placed in front of the desk. Carlos paces back and forth in the office, while Mr. Martinez is seated.)

MR. MARTINEZ: Carlos, for someone who isn't nervous, you're doing a very good imitation!

CARLOS: *(stops pacing)* Sorry, Dad. I guess this waiting is getting to me. I wonder what's taking Mr. Boswell so long? I'd kind of like to go to my new class and get the new boy routine over with.

(Mr. Boswell comes in and sits at his desk. Carlos also sits down.)

MR. BOSWELL: *(frowning)* We checked all our mail, and I'm sorry to say that Carlos's transcripts from Mexico City have not yet arrived.

CARLOS: *(aside to the audience, thinking aloud)* Great! That probably means I don't have to start school today.

MR. BOSWELL: However, I'm happy to say that Carlos can still start school today.

(Carlos's face falls.)

MR. MARTINEZ: Mr. Boswell, we haven't even received all the boxes with our household belongings from Mexico yet. I'm not surprised the transcripts

haven't arrived. But we're eager to get Carlos back into his classes, aren't we, Carlos?

CARLOS: *(turning to speak directly to audience in an aside)* I wouldn't exactly say "eager." *(to his father)* Yes, sir.

MR. BOSWELL: I'm surprised to learn that you are American citizens. We thought you were moving here from Mexico for the first time.

MR. MARTINEZ: My wife and I are from Mexico originally. We met in college here in the United States, and we decided to remain here. Carlos was born in America and lived here for almost nine years before we moved to Mexico City. In fact, we lived right in this area. We liked this part of the state, and we decided to return to it when I was transferred back to the United States.

MR. BOSWELL: Well, we're very glad you are joining us at Thomas Dewey, Carlos. You'll be in Mrs. Cabrero's homeroom. She'll also be your first-period Spanish teacher. So, we're all set. Why don't we go and meet your new classmates?

(They all walk toward the door. Carlos pulls his father back.)

CARLOS: *Papa, un momento, por favor.*

MR. MARTINEZ: Sure, *hijo*. Mr. Boswell, do you mind if Carlos and I talk privately for a minute?

MR. BOSWELL: No, of course not. Please, use my office. I'll wait for you in the hallway, Carlos.

CARLOS: Thank you, sir.

(Mr. Boswell leaves. Carlos slumps into a chair and exhales deeply.)

CARLOS: Promise me one thing, Dad. Then I'll be able to handle this a little better.

MR. MARTINEZ: *(concerned)* What is it, *hijo*? Tell me what I can do.

CARLOS: Promise me this will be the last time I have to be the new boy at school. Promise we'll stay where we are until I go to college.

MR. MARTINEZ: Carlos, I can't promise you that.

The one thing that's constant in life is change. Maybe it's easier to thrive when everything and everyone around you is familiar, but it's also good to know you can adapt and do well when changes come along.

CARLOS: Maybe that was my problem in my last two schools. It took a long time before I felt as if I fit in. Here, though, I do speak the language. I can blend in more easily.

MR. MARTINEZ: That's the spirit!

CARLOS: I guess I can try to be interested in the same things the kids here are interested in.

MR. MARTINEZ: *(encouragingly)* Sure you can.

CARLOS: Is it too much to hope that some kids will be interested in the same things that I like?

MR. MARTINEZ: Of course not, Carlos. I think kids are the same no matter where you are in the world. Besides, fitting in doesn't mean you have to change who you are.

(Carlos, after thinking a bit, looks up and nods at his father. He stands up, ready to face his new school.)

MR. MARTINEZ: *(smiles and pats Carlos on the back)* Okay, *hijo*. Have a great day! *(He goes offstage.)*

CARLOS: *(aside to the audience)* I don't think Dad really understands. My father has so many friends.

No matter where we live, people flock to see him. He's an architect, and they want him to design their department stores and office buildings. My mother is a doctor. Everywhere we go, people respect her. Me—I'm just an ordinary kid. I like to play baseball. I was pretty good at second base on my old team. I haven't played in three years, though. The fact is, there's nothing about me that will seem special to the kids here. They won't care that I know all about the Aztec culture. It's not as if there are ancient sites to visit around here. It's just going to be the new boy routine all over again.

Scene 4
Carlos the Goalie?

(Mrs. Cabrero's classroom, Monday morning. The banner that Cleo and Tasha hung on the wall on Friday is now sagging. While Mrs. Cabrero marks the attendance record, the students chat.)

CLEO: Has anyone seen Carlos yet?

TASHA: There was no sign of him when I passed the office this morning.

PAUL: I wonder why he's late?

VALERIE: Cleo, Tasha—look at your banner! It's falling down.

CLEO, TASHA: Oh, no!

TASHA: *(raising her hand)* Mrs. Cabrero, may Cleo and I go fix our banner?

MRS. CABRERO: Please do, Tasha.

(The two girls pop out of their seats to repair the sign. They fix it, then sit down again.)

PAUL: Malcolm, did you talk to Coach Jones about having the new boy join the soccer team?

MALCOLM: Coach said I should bring him to practice after school today. He says we'll play a scrimmage game, with Carlos as the goalkeeper.

PAUL: Great! With Carlos as your new goalie, you'll be unbeatable.

MRS. CABRERO: There, the attendance is done. Paul, would you take this down to the office, please? *(She raises her voice.)* Quiet down, class. I know everyone is excited about Carlos coming—

(Just then, Carlos and Mr. Boswell enter. All the students turn to look at them. Once Mrs. Cabrero realizes they have arrived, she stops talking.)

CARLOS: *(takes a deep breath, then talks in an aside to the audience)* There they are. Twenty pairs of eyes fixed on me, scrutinizing, judging, sizing me up.

MR. BOSWELL: Good morning, Mrs. Cabrero, class. Meet your new student, Carlos Martinez.

ALL STUDENTS: *(in a chorus of greetings)* ¡Buenos días, Carlos! ¡Bienvenidos, Carlos!

MRS. CABRERO: *Buenos días, Carlos.*

Bienvenidos a nuestra clase.

CARLOS: *(aside to audience)* Wow—I must have missed homeroom. This must be Spanish class already. I'd better answer in Spanish. *(to class and Mrs. Cabrero) Gracias, Señora Cabrero. Estoy contento de estar en los Estados Unidos.*

VALERIE: *(coming up to Carlos with her hand extended) Buenos días, Carlos. Me llamo Valerie. ¡Mucho gusto!*

CARLOS: *(wipes his sweaty palms on his pants and then shakes Val's hand) Mucho gusto, Valerie. Gracias.*

MALCOLM: *Hola, Carlos. Mi nombre es Malcolm. ¿Qué pasa, amigo?*

CARLOS: *(smiling for the first time) Hola, Malcolm. (pauses and gestures to the hat sticking out from Malcolm's desk) Me gusta su sombrero.*

MALCOLM: Sorry, Carlos, but Mrs. Cabrero didn't teach us that phrase yet!

MRS. CABRERO: He said . . .

CARLOS: Oh, I can say it in English if you'd like. *(to Malcolm)* I said I like your hat.

OTHER STUDENTS: What? He speaks English? Did you hear that?

MRS. CABRERO: *(surprised as well)* Carlos, you speak English very well.

MR. BOSWELL: Actually, Mrs. Cabrero, Carlos grew

up in the United States. His family moved to Mexico three years ago and now they've returned to the United States. I'm sorry we didn't know this sooner, but Carlos's records haven't arrived yet from his old school.

CLEO: (*sounding disappointed*) You mean you're not really from Mexico City?

CARLOS: Well, my parents were born in Mexico, but I only lived in Mexico City for three years. I'm really from around here. I lived in this part of the state until I was almost nine.

OTHER STUDENTS: (*expressing some disappointment*) Oh.

CARLOS: (*aside*) Uh-oh. What did I say wrong? I thought they'd like me more if they knew I was just like them!

MRS. CABRERO: We're glad to have Carlos join us, no matter where he's from, aren't we, class?

TASHA: Yes, Mrs. Cabrero. It's just that we worked so hard on the banner and everything. . . . We just thought—

OTHER STUDENTS: Sssh! Never mind!

MR. BOSWELL: (*exiting*) Good luck, Carlos.

MRS. CABRERO: Please take a seat, Carlos, wherever you'd like. As you can see, we have several empty desks you could take.

(*Carlos looks out over the available seats. As he does this, Cleo, Tasha, and Malcolm all try to pretend that they don't care whether or not Carlos sits next to them. Malcolm drums his fingers on his desk. Cleo looks away. Tasha shrugs.)*

CARLOS: *(aside)* No one wants to sit near me. They don't like me, I can tell. I'll just sit over on the side by myself.

(Carlos takes the nearest desk and chair, which is nowhere near Cleo, Tasha, or Malcolm. These three students exchange disappointed looks.)

CLEO: *(aside)* Humph! I wonder if he's a little bit of a snob, refusing to sit with the rest of us.

TASHA: *(also speaking her thoughts aloud)* Well, I guess he doesn't like us very much.

MALCOLM: *(speaking in a stage whisper to Paul)* Why did he sit way over there?

PAUL: I don't know!

VALERIE: Ssssh! He'll hear you. Don't scrutinize everything he does! You'll make him nervous.

MRS. CABRERO: Carlos, tell us a little about yourself.

CARLOS: *(stands awkwardly after just sitting down)* Si, Señora Cabrero. I mean, yes, Mrs. Cabrero. Well, I'm twelve. . . . *(aside)* What are you saying? Everyone knows that! You're in the sixth grade. Say something interesting. I could tell them that I like studying Aztec ruins, but probably nobody here has even heard of them. Then they'll really think I'm weird. What should I say? I know! I'll tell them I like playing second base. *(addresses the class again)* And I like playing sports, especially s—

MALCOLM: *(interrupting)* All right! You play soccer! I'll bet you're a great player. How about joining our team?

PAUL: Yeah, they need a new goalkeeper. Their best goalie moved away.

CARLOS: *(aside)* Soccer! I'm a terrible soccer player. My legs get tangled up with the ball, and I end up tripping on the field. But they want me to play on their team, and if I want to be accepted, I guess I should do what they want. *(To students)* Sure! I played soccer all the time in Mexico City. In fact, our team won the regional championship last year.

MALCOLM, PAUL: Yes!

MALCOLM: Carlos, there's a soccer practice after school today. Will you stay and work out with us?

CARLOS: *(hesitantly)* Uh—*(aside)* Today! What have I gotten myself into? Once I get on that field, everyone will see what a bad soccer player I am. *(to Malcolm)* I have to ask my parents if I can stay, but I'm sure it'll be okay.

PAUL: What position did you play in Mexico, Carlos?

CARLOS: *(aside)* What should I say? I mean, sure I played a little soccer in Mexico, but I didn't have a regular position. I wasn't even on a team!

MALCOLM: You weren't a goalie, were you?

CARLOS: Actually, that's exactly what I was. Yes, I was—I am—a goalie. *(aside)* In my dreams!

MALCOLM: You're just what the team needs—a soccer player from Mexico, where soccer is king. We'll be unbeatable!

(Malcolm gives Carlos a high-five. Carlos grins sheepishly and slaps Malcolm's hand. The other students applaud.)

TASHA: I'll come to the practice this afternoon, Carlos, to cheer you on.

CLEO: I'll come, too.

CARLOS: *(unenthusiastically)* Gee—thanks.

MALCOLM: The whole class should come to watch our super new player, Carlos Martinez!

(A bell rings.)

MRS. CABRERO: I'm glad that Carlos is going to play on your team, Malcolm. Now, class, we need to get started with our Spanish lesson. I have a workbook for you, Carlos. Let's all turn to chapter 10.

(Carlos stands up to take the book that Mrs. Cabrero is handing to him.)

CARLOS: *(aside) Ay yi yi yi yi! (He takes a deep breath.)* From second base *(he crouches down as if catching a ground ball)* to soccer goalie *(he gets into a goalkeeper's stance)* in one short morning. I can't wait to tell Dad just how adaptable I can be!

Scene 5
Misconceptions

(The school cafeteria at lunchtime. Cleo and Tasha enter, pick up lunch trays, and get in line. They face the audience as if that is where the serving area is located, and they move along, pretending to take silverware and milk as though they are progressing in the line. Behind them, several other students are seated at a table. They pantomime eating, talking, and laughing throughout the scene.)

CLEO: I just don't think Carlos likes us very much. He barely said a word to me when I told him I would come to the soccer practice. He wouldn't even look at me when it was time to choose a desk.

TASHA: He didn't look at me, either.

CLEO: Did you notice that he never said one word about our gorgeous banner?

TASHA: Yes. What did we do wrong?

CLEO: *(looks up to order and speaks to an unseen cafeteria worker)* I'll have a chicken wrap and a salad, please. No tomato on the wrap, if you don't mind. Does the salad have iceberg lettuce or romaine? No croutons, thanks. Do you have any Parmesan cheese?

TASHA: Mrs. Cabrero assigned Valerie to show Carlos where his other classes are. He's clinging to Val as if she were a lifeline. I think Mrs. Cabrero should have assigned Carlos to go to classes with one of us, don't you?

CLEO: Yes, definitely. At least we're all in Spanish class together, though.

TASHA: *(ordering)* I'll have a slice of pizza, please. Thank you.

(Paul enters the line, picks up a tray, and looks hungrily at the menu.)

PAUL: They have chiliburgers—my favorite!

CLEO: Paul, any kind of food is your favorite food. Guacamole, chiliburgers—it's all the same to you!

TASHA: You know, I've been wondering something. Why would a boy who lived in Mexico for three years need to take a Spanish class?

30

PAUL: He takes it for the same reason we have to study English.

CLEO: That makes sense. We've been speaking English all our lives, but we still need to learn about vocabulary and literature and everything.

PAUL: *(ordering enthusiastically)* Yes, ma'am. I'd like a double-cheese chiliburger. Could I get two side orders of corn with that? Do you have any hot sauce? And, let's see, fresh fruit. . . do we just get one piece?

CLEO: I don't really care why he's in our Spanish class. I just want to know why he won't talk to us.

TASHA: Maybe he's shy.

(Just then, Valerie enters the line. She pantomimes reaching for a milk carton, then moves toward the end of the line. She notices the others looking at her questioningly and holds up a brown bag.)

VALERIE: I brought my lunch today.

(The others nod.)

CLEO: So, Val—you've spent all morning with Carlos. Tell us about him.

VALERIE: He's very polite, but he hasn't said much. He seems kind of nervous, actually, though I guess that's to be expected.

TASHA: Does he like us or not?

CLEO: Does he want to be our friend?

VALERIE: Give it a rest! It's his first day. He just

31

met us this morning. Let's give him time to decide whom he wants to be friends with.

(Malcolm enters the line and gets a tray.)

MALCOLM: *(ordering)* I'll have a burger, please. Hold the cheese and chili. Could I get some corn, too?

PAUL: Is that all you're eating?

MALCOLM: *(ignores Paul)* Hey, Val, where is my man, Carlos?

VALERIE: He had to report to the office before lunch. I think his records finally turned up. He'll be here soon.

MALCOLM: Good. When he comes in, we'll sit him down, and I'll give him a briefing about our team. In four weeks, we play Central, and this year, with Carlos's help, we can win!

CLEO: Soccer, soccer—that's all you talk about, Malcolm. Tasha and I want Carlos to sit with us and tell us about Mexico City.

PAUL: I agree with Malcolm. With Carlos's skills, Thomas Dewey Middle School has a chance to be a championship team, just like the one he left.

VALERIE: Maybe Carlos wants to eat and not talk at all! Did you ever think of that?

TASHA: That's ridiculous, Val! Why would he do that when he could be talking to us?

VALERIE: All of you have preconceived notions

about Carlos. That's all I'm saying.

CLEO: All right! We'll let Carlos decide where he wants to sit and what he wants to talk about. *(taking her order)* I'll get us a table.

TASHA: *(also taking her order)* I'll make sure we have a chair for Carlos.

PAUL: *(picking up his meal)* Just leave me enough elbow room to eat!

VALERIE: With all that food, you may need a table to yourself, Paul.

PAUL: Baseball season is starting soon. I'll need my strength!

MALCOLM: *(grumbling to himself as he receives his order)* Of course soccer is all I talk about. I'm going to play in the World Cup tournament one day. I have to stay focused!

(They all exit offstage. Seconds later, Carlos enters and looks around.)

CARLOS: *(aside)* There are Malcolm and the others. How can I face them after that big story I told? They'll want to ask me a lot of questions about my "championship team." Maybe I should just tell everyone the truth right now and clear this up. That might settle the butterflies in my stomach.

MALCOLM: *(from offstage)* Hey, Carlos! We're over here!

CARLOS: *(gives a halfhearted wave)* Oh, no—

they saw me! I'm in trouble now! Every time I open my mouth, I say something wrong or I say something untrue. If I can hurry through the line, maybe I can get to another table before they come over here. *(He gets in line, picks up a tray, and moves along the line to order.)*

CARLOS: I'm so nervous, I probably won't be able to eat a single—*(his eyes light up at the sight of pizza)* SLICE OF PIZZA! *(to cafeteria worker)* I'd like two slices, please. *(He takes his order and goes over to sit at the table with the other students.)*

OTHER STUDENTS: Hi!

CARLOS: Hi. *(He takes a big bite of pizza, as if he doesn't want to talk. After a moment, the other students shrug and then continue laughing and talking.)*

CARLOS: *(aside)* I know I should try to be friendly, but right now, I'm so confused I don't think I could get my own name straight. This day is turning into one big catastrophe!

(Cleo and Tasha return onstage and put their trays on a stand.)

TASHA: Hey, there's Carlos. He's sitting over there with some other kids.

CLEO: I wonder why he's doing that?

TASHA: *(sadly)* I guess he doesn't like us.

(Malcolm enters and puts his tray on the stand.)

MALCOLM: Where did Carlos go?

CLEO: *(points)* He's sitting over there.

TASHA: It was as if he didn't want to have anything to do with us. What would make him act that way?

CLEO: I don't know. Come on, let's go to the gym and shoot some hoops.

(Cleo exits, and Tasha follows. Malcolm remains a few moments more, with a skeptical look toward Carlos. Shaking his head in confusion, he turns and exits.)

Scene 6
We're a Team, Right?

(A soccer field, that afternoon. The field can be suggested, rather than created with props. Cleo and Tasha enter and move to one side of the stage.)

CLEO: Where is everyone?

TASHA: There are Paul and Valerie. Hey, over here! *(Tasha waves to Paul and Valerie, who join Cleo and Tasha onstage.)*

CLEO: Here comes the team now.

(Coach Jones enters, with a whistle in his hand. He blows it, and Malcolm and Carlos run out onto the stage wearing soccer shorts and shirts. They jog in place.)

VALERIE: *(calling out to the players and clapping her hands)* Come on team, let's move it! Let's get out there and show some spirit. You've got to run faster, dribble better, and make those goals! Come on, team, give it all you've got!

COACH JONES: *(gruffly)* Valerie . . .

VALERIE: Yes, Coach?

COACH JONES: It's only a practice match.

VALERIE: *(grinning)* I know, Coach. But don't you think the team needs a little moral support?

COACH JONES: Fine. Keep it up, Valerie! Okay,

team, we're going to play a scrimmage game today.

MALCOLM, CARLOS: Yes, Coach!

COACH JONES: *(to Carlos)* Carlos? I hear you're a goalie. Malcolm tells me you played some championship soccer where you came from.

(Carlos hesitates, and the coach raises his eyebrows.)

COACH JONES: You did play soccer in Mexico City, right?

CARLOS: Uh—yes, Coach! *(aside)* Just not much!

COACH JONES: Okay, let's see what you can do. We'll play jerseys against T-shirts. Get to your starting positions!

MALCOLM, CARLOS: Yes, Coach! *(They turn to each other.)* ¡Campeones, campeones, ra, ra, ra!

TASHA, CLEO: Hey, what's that cheer?

MALCOLM: Carlos taught it to us in the locker room. *Campeones* means "champions."

TASHA, CLEO, VALERIE, PAUL: ¡Campeones, campeones, ra, ra, ra!

(Malcolm and Carlos start to move forward, toward the audience.)

COACH JONES: Carlos!

CARLOS: Yes, Coach?

COACH JONES: *(pointing toward the back of the stage)* The goal is over there.

(Carlos, embarrassed, turns and goes the other way. Malcolm runs back to him.)

MALCOLM: Carlos, are you okay?

CARLOS: Well, um . . . truthfully, Malcolm . . .

(Malcolm waits for an answer.)

CARLOS: *(aside)* It's too late now to tell Malcolm that I've never been a goalie. If I tell him the truth, he'll hate me for sure, after he went to the trouble of asking Coach Jones to give me a shot. So—I'd better just go along for now. Carlos Martinez, instant goalkeeper. *(to Malcolm)* Sure, I'm fine!

MALCOLM: Great! We're a team, right? Let's go make this happen.

CARLOS: Right!

(Carlos goes to stand at the back of the stage, facing the audience. Malcolm returns to center stage. His actions should reflect Carlos's narration of the soccer game. As Carlos narrates, the fans on the sidelines pantomime watching the game and reacting to the plays.)

CARLOS: *(looking at center stage with apprehension)* What have I gotten myself into? I've never played this position in my life. Why did I tell that big lie? Now look where it's gotten me. (*He glances over at the fans and coach on the sidelines.*) Everyone thinks I'm a great soccer player. They're over there, ready to cheer for me. By the time this is all over, they'll be laughing at me, no doubt about it. *(He shades his eyes and peers at Malcolm.)* Then there's Malcolm. He's counting on me to be a valuable player. I feel terrible about that. He seems like somebody who could be a good friend. Oh, no! There's the kickoff! *(he gets into the goalkeeper's stance)* The ball is in play. With any luck, it'll never come anywhere near me. Oh, please, don't come my way! Look, Malcolm's got control of the ball. Look at him go! He's dribbling down the field. He's going for the attack! All right, Malcolm, take it all the way! All the way to the other side of the field. *¡Ra, ra, ra!*

PAUL: *(calling out)* Watch out, Malcolm! Look behind you!

CARLOS: Oh, no! Those two boys are gaining on Malcolm. They're double-teaming him. It's a battle for the ball. Uh-oh! They intercepted! *(panicking)* And they're coming this way! No! Malcolm, stop them!

VALERIE: *(shouting)* Come on, Malcolm!

CARLOS: Oh, no, they're in the box. Jerseys! Get the ball away! The T-shirts' forward is moving into position! He kicks! Oh, no! It's coming at me like a speeding bullet! Aghhhhh!

(In a frenzy, Carlos catches the ball and falls to the ground, the wind knocked out of him.)

COACH JONES: *(blows his whistle)* Save!

(The fans break into wild cheers.)

CLEO, TASHA, VALERIE, PAUL: *¡Campeones, campeones, ra, ra, ra!*

(Panting, Carlos lifts his head and realizes he has prevented the point. Malcolm raises his fists over his shoulders.)

MALCOLM: Nice save, Carlos!

STUDENTS: Go, Carlos!

VALERIE: Carlos, Carlos, he's our man! If he can't do it, nobody can! *¡Ra, ra, ra!*

(Carlos grins widely as the coach blows his whistle for the next play. Carlos throws the ball into play and returns to his position defending the goal.)

CARLOS: *(aside)* Wow! I did it. I made a save! How in the world did I do that? Oh, well, that doesn't matter. Everybody saw it, and they think I'm great! They like me!

(He goes back into the goalkeeper's stance.)

CARLOS: The ball is in play again. Jerseys have the ball. They're passing successfully, moving down the field. Yes! Malcolm has the ball again. He fakes to the left; he glides to the right. Uh-oh, here come the two guards again, gaining on him. But—oh! He rushes past them! Malcolm's on his own—he's going for the goal. He kicks. It sails over the goalie's head!

COACH: Goal!

(Again, there are cheers and whistles from the

sidelines. Carlos runs to greet Malcolm, who is returning to his team's side.)

MALCOLM: *(to Carlos)* We're a team, all right. We're unstoppable!

(Coach blows his whistle and waves his arms toward the two boys.)

COACH: Enough clowning around, boys. Ball is in play!

(Malcolm trots back to centerfield. Carlos struts back to his position with a little bit of a swagger in his manner.)

CARLOS: *(aside)* Being the new kid isn't so bad if you can get everyone to like you on your first day. Even if you're pretending to be someone you're not. Look at me—I'm a real soccer hero. Malcolm and I are a team! Everyone's cheering for the team, for me! For—oomph!

(Carlos yelps as the ball hits his face, and he falls to the ground. He crouches over and holds his hands up to his face.)

CARLOS: Oooh! My nose! Ooooh!

(Everyone runs to his side.)

VALERIE: Player down!

PAUL: He's hurt, Coach.

TASHA: Oh, no!

CLEO: Someone help him!

(Carlos continues to moan in pain.)

COACH JONES: *(coming to check on Carlos)* Let me see, Carlos.

CARLOS: It's broken. My nose is broken!

(Coach Jones looks at Carlos's face, which is blocked from the audience's view. Coach hands Carlos a towel.)

COACH JONES: Here, hold this under your nose, Carlos. Come with me to my office. We need to call your parents.

CARLOS: Okay, Coach. *(aside)* I can't believe it! I got hit in the face by the ball right in front of everyone. It's all my fault, pretending to be a goalie! Now my nose is broken, and I'll never be able to show my face in this school again! If they weren't going to make fun of me before, they surely will now.

COACH JONES: Come on Carlos, let's get you to the office. Clear the way, everyone!

(The Coach leads Carlos out. The other students follow somberly.)

Scene 7
Carlos Tells the Truth

(The hall outside the coach's office, that afternoon. This can be suggested by an empty stage and a sign near the stage exit that says PHYS ED OFFICE. Valerie, Paul, Tasha, Cleo, and Malcolm stand near the exit, as if that is the door to the coach's office. They all appear very concerned.)

MALCOLM: Did anyone see what happened?

PAUL: Sure—he got knocked in the face by a 15-pound ball.

VALERIE: I don't know what he was watching, but it wasn't the ball. Malcolm, I wonder how much experience Carlos has had playing that position.

MALCOLM: He did make a great save.

VALERIE: That's true, but an experienced goalie would never have taken his eyes off the ball.

TASHA: Do you think his nose is really broken?

PAUL: It looked like some serious damage to me.

MALCOLM: Will it keep him from playing in the regionals?

VALERIE: Malcolm, can you stop thinking about soccer for one minute? Our new friend is hurt!

CLEO: Dr. Martinez has been in there with Carlos for a long time.

MALCOLM: I know his mom's a doctor, but wouldn't she take Carlos to a hospital if he was *seriously* injured—if he was hurt so badly that he couldn't play soccer?

VALERIE: Malcolm, tell me the truth. Do you care more about how Carlos is or about the future of your soccer team?

MALCOLM: *(looking hurt)* Of course I care more about how Carlos is!

VALERIE: Well then, stop talking about the soccer team!

PAUL: *(peeking through the glass in the door)* Here they come now.

(Carlos, Coach Jones, and Dr. Isabel Martinez come onstage. Dr. Martinez carries a black doctor's case. Carlos holds an ice bag over one side of his face.)

DR. MARTINEZ: I'm happy to report there are no broken bones. Just a cut and a big bruise.

CLEO, PAUL, VALERIE, MALCOLM, TASHA: Great! Yeah!

DR. MARTINEZ: He'll have to keep that ice on the bruise until the swelling goes down. Then he'll be as good as new.

MALCOLM: *(steps up to Carlos)* It's tough getting hit in the face on your first day of school.

CARLOS: *(ruefully)* That isn't my only problem, Malcolm.

MALCOLM: What? What do you mean?

(Carlos looks at his mother, who nods. Carlos looks back at his classmates.)

CARLOS: Well, there's something I need to explain.

(Carlos looks at his mother again, takes a deep breath, and then comes out with it.)

CARLOS: I exaggerated my soccer skills this morning. *(pauses)* I was never on the regional soccer championship team in Mexico. I was never on a winning team at all. In fact, I only played a little soccer with my friends in Mexico—and then I wasn't any good at it. My real game is baseball. I like to play second base.

(The other students exchange looks of surprise.)

VALERIE: *(to the other students)* I told you we shouldn't assume he could play soccer just because he was from Mexico! Did anyone listen?

MALCOLM: He could have just told us he wasn't much of a soccer player. *(to Carlos)* Why'd you make up that story about how you'd played on a winning team?

CARLOS: *(contritely)* I thought if I joined the team you'd . . . well, that you'd accept me and I wouldn't have to go through the new boy routine. Now, I wouldn't be surprised if you wanted nothing more to do with me. I'll always be an outsider, the kid who lied to you.

(The other students exchange looks.)

CARLOS: I'm sorry, everyone.

(The other students' expressions turn thoughtful.)

VALERIE: I understand why you did what you did, Carlos. I think we should start all over again in homeroom tomorrow morning

PAUL: *(after a moment)* Do I ever know what the new boy routine is. When I came to this school, I was so nervous! I'd played baseball at my old school, but I knew I'd have to try out for the team all over again here. I'm just glad that people here at Thomas Dewey were nice to me. It could have been very hard. *(He points to Cleo and Tasha.)* Although I remember that you two tried so hard to make me feel welcome that it was kind of unnerving!

CLEO: What?

TASHA: *(indignantly)* That was just your imagination!

(They all turn to Malcolm, who is frowning slightly. Then, looking at Carlos, he smiles.)

MALCOLM: *(apologetically)* I put you on the spot, asking you to join our team like that. I thought you were telling us you played soccer, and I never really gave you a chance to say no. *(He thinks about it.)* I guess you've suffered enough for telling us about your nonexistent soccer career. Carlos, it took courage to stand in front of that goal. You're pretty brave.

(The other students nod in agreement.)

PAUL: I'm glad to hear your real game is baseball.

CARLOS: I used to play second base back when I was in third grade. I'd like to try again, if that's all right with you, Coach Jones.

COACH: Come to the tryouts, Carlos. I'll be glad to see how you play.

CARLOS: *(grinning widely)* Gracias, amigos.

MALCOLM: *De nada. (He holds out his hand, and Carlos shakes it.)*

CLEO: If we're going to start all over again tomorrow morning, can you look at the banner that Tasha and I made for you? It says "*¡Bienvenidos, Carlos!*" in big letters—

TASHA: With pictures of Mexico City!

CARLOS: Sure, I'll look out for it.

VALERIE: You'd better appreciate that banner, or we'll never hear the end of it!

(Everyone laughs. The other students leave, calling their good-byes. Carlos and his mother walk slowly toward the exit with Coach Jones.)

DR. MARTINEZ: Are you feeling better, Carlos?

CARLOS: Mom, I feel better than I have since we moved back to America. Just imagine, I got the whole new boy routine over with in one disastrous day.

DR. MARTINEZ: Yes, although you chose a very unusual way to accomplish that!

COACH JONES: The students here at Thomas Dewey really are very friendly, Carlos. I think you're going to like it here.

CARLOS: Thanks, Coach. I like it here already.

(They exit.)

Scene 8
Play the Game You Know

(Mrs. Cabrero's homeroom, the next day. Mrs. Cabrero is seated at her desk, taking attendance. Cleo and Tasha stand under the banner, smiling anxiously. Carlos arrives onstage and pauses in the doorway. He now wears a bandage over one side of his nose.)

CARLOS: *(clutching his heart)* Wow, there's the famous banner! How could I have missed it yesterday? It's beautiful! It must have taken you hours to make!

CLEO: Did you notice the lettering?

TASHA: Do you recognize the scenes of Mexico City?

CARLOS: All this and scenes of Mexico City too? I'll have to take a closer look. (*He crosses the stage to look at the banner.*)

VALERIE: (*entering*) I had a feeling you'd like that banner!

(*Paul, Malcolm, and the other students enter and sit down at their desks as Mrs. Cabrero continues marking the attendance sheet.*)

MRS. CABRERO: (*standing in front of her desk*) Please take your seats, everyone. I need to finish taking attendance. Carlos, I heard that you had an eventful soccer practice yesterday. I'm glad to see that you're not seriously hurt.

CARLOS: Just my honor, Mrs. Cabrero. That was an experiment that I've decided not to repeat.

(*Malcolm, Paul, Cleo, Tasha, and Valerie grin as the bell rings.*)

MRS. CABRERO: All right then, class. I want to know what topics you'd like to explore for our end-of-the-year project. You know the sixth-grade Spanish class always has a fantastic entry in our Language Fair. In the past we've learned songs in Spanish and put on skits.What are your ideas?

(*Cleo raises her hand.*)

MRS. CABRERO: Yes, Cleo?

CLEO: Mrs. Cabrero, because we have someone in our class who has lived in Mexico City, I say let's make an exhibit about Mexico City for our project.

OTHER STUDENTS: That's a great idea! Sure, Carlos can help us!

MRS. CABRERO: There seems to be general agreement. But Mexico City is a broad topic, Cleo. Let's try to be more specific. What is it about the culture that you want to know more about?

CLEO: The famous writers!

TASHA: The art!

VALERIE, MALCOLM, PAUL: The sports!

OTHER STUDENTS: The food! What are their schools like? What do kids do for fun?

(The questions become a buzz of sound. Then Carlos slowly raises his hand.)

MRS. CABRERO: Yes, Carlos? Why don't you stand up and tell us your idea.

CARLOS: *(standing)* Mexico City is a modern city— the capital of Mexico. But what I liked most about living there is that Mexico City is built on the site of Tenochtitlán, the capital of the ancient Aztec Empire. You can still see some of the ruins of the civilization. *(speaking more rapidly as he grows excited about his subject)* Did you know the Zócalo, the big public square in Mexico City, has been the center of the city ever since Aztec times? You can see important objects from the excavations done there in the Templo Mayor Museum. I visited all of the sites I

could while I was there—the temples, the pyramids—

MALCOLM: *(interrupting)* Pyramids? You mean like the ones in Egypt?

PAUL: There are pyramids in Mexico?

CARLOS: Sure! I've got pictures and maps and a model of the entire city the way it looked in Aztec times. I could bring them to class if you want me to.

PAUL: That would be perfect for our exhibit!

CLEO: Remember when we learned about the Aztecs in social studies?

TASHA: They had beautiful sculptures, didn't they?

MALCOLM: We can find out even more about the

Aztec culture. It's really interesting.

VALERIE: Maybe we could make Aztec headdresses and wear them on the day of the Language Fair.

PAUL: We can serve the foods they ate back then. Do you think they ate guacamole?

(The students begin to talk over each other in their enthusiasm for this topic.)

MRS. CABRERO: Then it's agreed. We'll study the Aztec civilization that existed where Mexico City is today.

CLASS: Yeah!

(Excited talk continues among the students. Carlos steps out of their midst to speak to the audience. The students can either freeze or fall into pantomime during Carlos's aside.)

CARLOS: *(to audience)* Who would have thought that the subject I like to talk about most is what's got everyone so excited? *(he shrugs)* I guess my dad was right. Even when things change, and you have to start all over again in a new place, that doesn't mean you have to change who you are. *(He pauses.)* Here's some advice. If you ever move to a new town, and you're the new kid in school, try *not* to assume that people aren't going to accept you. Give them a chance.

(Carlos starts to return to the group, but doubles back.)

CARLOS: Here's some more advice. Don't pretend to be someone you're not just to make people like you. Play the game you know. *(Carlos again starts back, then stops.)* Oh, and one more thing. Whenever you see something coming at you really fast—*(shouting)* DUCK! *(He ducks out of the way of an imaginary ball. Then, laughing, he rejoins the other students.)*

Glossary of Spanish Phrases

adiós	*good-bye*
amigo	*friend*
bienvenidos a nuestra clase	*welcome to our class*
buenos días	*good day*
campeones, campeones, ra, ra, ra	*champions, champions, ra, ra, ra*
¿Cómo estás?	*How are you?*
de nada	*you're welcome*
Estoy contento de estar en los Estados Unidos.	*I am pleased to be in the United States.*
fútbol	*soccer*
gracias	*thank you*
hijo	*son*
hola	*hello*
Me gusta su sombrero.	*I like your hat.*
me llamo	*my name is*
mi nombre es	*my name is*
mucho gusto	*nice to meet you*
Museo Nacional de Antropología	*National Anthropology Museum*
muy bien, gracias	*very well, thank you*
¿Qué pasa?	*What's happening?*
si	*yes*
Señora	*Mrs.*
un momento, por favor	*one moment, please*